VICTORIOUS VICTORIANS

A GUIDE TO THE MAJOR ARCHITECTURAL STYLES

A GUIDE
TO THE MAJOR ARCHITECTURAL STYLES

VICTORIOUS VICTORIANS

TEXT BY

PEG B. SINCLAIR

PHOTOGRAPHS BY

TAYLOR B. LEWIS

An Owl Book

HOLT, RINEHART AND WINSTON
NEW YORK

Our thanks to many Historic Preservation officers, their assistants, and private restoration enthusiasts, who gave directions to Victorian houses throughout the country; to Tom and Sue Carroll of the Mainstay Inn in Cape May; to Greg Hadley, our photographic assistant throughout the rush to beat the fading light; to Ken Mills, Ellen and Lloyd Wells, Charles A. Johnson, and Carmelita and Taylor Lewis, Sr., who gave refuge along the long, harried route of Victorian America.

Text copyright © 1985 by Peg Sinclair
Photographs copyright © 1985 by Taylor Lewis

Published by Holt, Rinehart and Winston,
383 Madison Avenue, New York, New York 10017.

Published simultaneously in Canada by Holt, Rinehart and Winston of Canada, Limited.

Library of Congress Cataloging in Publication Data

Sinclair, Peg B.
  Victorious Victorians.

    "An Owl book."
    Bibliography: p.
    1. Wooden-frame houses—United States.
  2. Architecture, Victorian—United States. I. Lewis,
Taylor Biggs. II. Title.
NA7207.S56 1985   728.3'7'0973   85-7612
  ISBN 0-03-004063-9 (pbk.)

First Edition

Designer: Taylor Lewis Associates
Printed in Japan
10 9 8 7 6 5 4 3 2 1

ISBN 0-03-004063-9

CONTENTS

Nowhere else in American history has the house form been so richly intricate as during the Victorian period, circa 1840–1910. At no other time was there such a wide choice in style and color.

Carpenter's lace on porches, balconies, and verandas; roof lines sporting cupolas, towers, turrets, finials, and spires; an array of exterior adornment—shingles of many shapes, patterned roof tiles, belt courses, brackets, bays, dentils, friezes, and porticos—all of these elements combined to present a many-splendored portrait known as the Mauve Decades.

Originating in Great Britain and named for Queen Victoria, this new architectural style began as a revolt against classic architectural forms.

After English wit and self-styled architect Hugh Walpole built his rambling Gothic Revival estate, Strawberry Hill, he entertained himself and the nation by visiting and criticizing other British Gothic Revival homes.

Said Walpole, "One has the satisfaction of imprinting the gloom of abbeys and cathedrals on one's house." In a letter to a friend he wrote, "I am almost as fond of the Sharawaggi or Chinese want of symmetry in buildings as in grounds or gardens. . . . You will be pleased by the liberty of taste . . . of which you can have no idea." He admonished his countrymen about Greek Revival architecture, saying that the classical style was dull and proper, and only for public buildings, not houses.

Gothic Revival, the earliest of the Victorian styles, began in America about 1840. It was inspired by the British movement but clearly adapted to American tastes and landscapes. Each of the major styles, in fact, was simplified and transformed to suit the land-rich, independent nation.

The Industrial Revolution in both England and the United States made available to the common people a previously unheard of wealth of goods, machinery, natural resources, and income. Wood was both plentiful and cheap, glass became readily available, and the invention of wood-cutting and -carving tools enabled the production of extraordinary embellishments to exteriors and interiors of houses. Indoor plumbing, central heating, and, finally, electricity were revolutionary creature comforts, introduced in the last quarter of the nineteenth century. Balloon construction, a new method of building, allowed faster and less expensive completion of each dwelling. For the very first time, an emerging middle class could afford to "do their own thing."

Much of the building philosophy of the time originated from John Ruskin's *The Seven Lamps of Architecture*, an ode to house form written in 1848. He stressed the beauty of shapes in nature and advocated the use of previously accepted house styles; and the Victorians followed his lead. His next book, *The Stones of Venice*, contained an admiring description of medieval architecture that led his followers to Gothic imitations, or the Gothic Revival style.

Andrew Jackson Downing, another major influence of the same decade, was a gifted landscape architect, who wrote *Victorian Cottage Residences* and *The Architecture of Country Houses*. A pioneer of the small dwelling in a country setting, he has been called the "father of the American suburb." His works were enriched with the illustrations of the architect Alexander Jackson Davis, author of *Rural Residences*.

Davis provided mail-order plans that could be followed by carpenters anywhere in America. These pattern books were printed and circulated with floor plans and prices included. Other Victorian house designers followed suit, reaching back to earlier architectural creations and adapting and refining many different house plans. Before long, catalogs were offering completed houses for $800 to $3,000.

But of all the Victorian authors and architects, many self-styled, no one was more captivating than the phrenologist Orson S. Fowler, author of *The Octagon House: A Home for All*. This book, which presented plans for comfortable living, created an instant fad for eight-sided houses, which continued for twenty years. Fowler's own Octagon house was a massive sixty-room structure on the Hudson River. His idea was that the octagon shape was closest to nature's finest design, the circle. A champion of easy living, he advocated dumbwaiters, speaking tubes, hot-air and hot-water furnaces, and that novelty, the indoor water closet. His ideas were incorporated in succeeding Victorian pattern books. And, in America, the search for creature comforts has never ended.

The majority of remaining grand old Victorians today are the popular and bewitching Queen Annes, the style that echoed the era's More Is Better motto.

The Queen Anne house was heavily adorned with bays, towers, decorative shingles, balconies, turrets, belt courses, and more.

Other Victorian styles gained popularity: the distinguished flat-roofed, bracketed Italianates; the French mansard roof of the Second Empire; the exterior framework lines of the Stick style; and the amusing Exotic Revivals, which included Swiss Chalet, Oriental, and Egyptian adaptations. The soaring high-arched Gothic Revivals and rare museumlike Octagons were considered the finest forms of their day.

Within the major styles mentioned, there was a good deal of cross-pollination, with features of one added to another. Gothic Revival lancet windows appeared in Italianate villas, Stick-style beams framed parts of Queen Annes, and so on.

The Folk Victorian house form, a recently devised category that may not be a style at all, has been presented as a catchall term for smaller box or railroad houses with mild Victorian decoration of any kind added. This type of house was often an earlier building updated with gingerbread trim on the porch.

There is, also, the occasional Colonial or Federal house, which has been transformed to a true Victorian style with extensive remodeling and proper additions.

The final style, the Shingle house, was a whimper of legendary Victorian ebullience. A sprawling bungalow-type house without ornamentation of any kind, this Spartan wood-shingled structure was first common at seaside resorts before spreading to other areas throughout the country.

The era ended with copies, rather than adaptations, of pure architectural styles which were rendered in masonry, brick, or brick veneer.

The finest examples of each Victorian style are today being preserved and restored. The growing admiration for Victorian house styles has influenced the builders and architects of today, who are providing modern Victorian adaptations along with restorations in suburban and city developments. Today's copies of what were originally adaptations themselves are a high compliment to a rich architectural heritage. It is a salute to a style of life many of us would love to emulate.

T H E
CHANGING DRESS
OF VICTORIAN COTTAGES:
C O L O R

The form of a house can be its art. It speaks of innermost delights and desires. Its exterior decorations and colors wave flags of meaning to those who can translate the signals.

. . . when the sun breaks out in gleams, there is something that delights and surprises in seeing an object, before only visible, lighted up in splendor, and then gradually sinking into shade; but a whitened object is already lighted up; it remains so when everything else has retired into obscurity; it still forces itself into notice, still impudently stares you in the face. An object of sober tint, unexpectedly gilded by the sun, is like a serious countenance suddenly lighted up by a smile; a whitened object like the eternal grin of a fool.

—"Essays on the Picturesque" by Uvedale Price as quoted in *Victorian Cottage Residences* by A. J. Downing, 1853

Indeed, the Victorians shunned white. A. J. Downing ranted, "[White] is too glowing and conspicuous. We scarcely know anything more uncomfortable to the eye than to approach the sunny side of a house in one of our brilliant midsummer days when it revels in the fashionable purity of its color. It is absolutely painful." In his books of the period, he advised paint shades that matched nature—the earth, rocks, wood, or the bark of trees—"fawn, drab, grey, brown." He also suggested that small cottages needed lighter colors for liveliness and that larger houses should be painted in more somber tones to express dignity.

The trend moved from Downing's pale colors to ever-darkening shades, and by 1870 to 1880, there were deep reds, olives, and dark-green dwellings, as well as the original lighter tones. By 1890, however, houses returned to pastels.

The Victorians were not the first to have their houses highly decorated in a variety of colors. One needs only to look at the magnificent Egyptian friezes, the Aztec and Mayan flair for decorations, or the Roman and Greek buildings to appreciate the long tradition of color. The Parthenon, that celebrated classic Greek temple whose remains are a pilgrimage for many, was brightly painted in the fourth century B.C.

Both light earth tones and deeper hues were the authentic dress of Victorian houses. Many of these colors have been faithfully applied to authentically preserved villas and cottages today, and Victorian houses are being repainted with verve.

The recent colorist movement in San Francisco has given new life to rich decoration, not only in California, but throughout the country. The Bay City has more surviving Victorian houses, some 16,000, than any other city in America; half of these have been restored. The move back to color, in the sixties, may have been a reaction to the gray and white paint that afflicted the Italianate, Stick, and Queen Anne styles of San Francisco during World War I and World War II.

California colors, bright, ornamental, and striking, are being used on houses everywhere. Talented Bay City specialists are being consulted on body and trim tones for Victorian residences in each region of the country; the West Coast example is luring new buyers to restore and repaint the grand old ladies of a bygone era. Preservationists have adapted the name "painted ladies" from a book of the same title to refer to the improper, tart dress of the colorist houses in contrast to the classic, subdued earth tones.

Key West, Florida; Cape May, New Jersey; and many other towns and cities have approved expanded palettes of colors for their historic districts. Each year, new paint adds pleasant surprises along the North Atlantic seacoast, where many Victorians abound.

Both the authentic earth-tone shades and the present more colorful trend are included in this book. For a look at true preservation colors, see *Century of Color* by Roger W. Moss, Ph.D., of the Philadelphia Athenaeum Museum.

Either color style, bright or subdued, is a matter of individual taste, which is, after all, what Victorian architecture is all about.

HOW TO
USE THIS BOOK

This book is a portrayal of the major American Victorian cottage styles. It is to be used as an identification field guide while touring, or as a guide while restoring and painting your very own Victorian house.

The various cottages, country homes, and villas were constructed primarily of wood; therefore brick, stone, masonry, and stucco are not included in this guide.

We have decided to eliminate the fancy châteaus and mansions beyond the reach of most of us; and, because wood was the prevalent Victorian building material, this book excludes the Richardson Romanesque style (1880–1900), a solid mass of masonry and stone, from these discussions of style and color.

The illustrations, with captions to direct attention to specific Victorian features, will assist the reader in his or her quest for an understanding of the Victorian spirit reflected in the houses of the era.

Further assistance may be obtained from the Glossary and Suggested Readings at the end of this book.

We would like to recommend *A Field Guide to American Houses* by Virginia and Lee McAlester for further study. Our handbook follows the style time periods outlined by the McAlesters' manual.

There are many wonderful Victorian examples that could not be included in this book. Most American towns today display at least one Victorian-style house. Look at them closely. Each has a story to tell.

GOTHIC REVIVAL

It is that strange disquietude of the Gothic spirit that is its greatness; that restlessness of the dreaming mind, that wanders hither and thither among the niches, and flickers feverishly around the pinnacles, and frets and fades in labyrinthine knots and shadows along wall and roof, and yet is not satisfied, nor shall be satisfied. The Greek could stay in his triglyph furrow, and be at peace; but the work of the Gothic heart is fretwork still, and it can neither rest in, nor from, its labour, but must pass on, sleeplessly, until its love of change shall be pacified forever in the change that must come alike on them that wake and them that sleep.

—John Ruskin, *The Stones of Venice*, 1851

To identify a Gothic Revival cottage, look for steeply pitched gable roofs. Pointed front-gable arches are trimmed with decorative, often flamboyant, vergeboard (or bargeboard) along the edge. A variety of windows such as lancet, trefoil, or oriel is common in such residences. Pointed dormer windows often have vergeboard trim.

Wooden board-and-batten siding, which is small vertical planks covering the joining line of wider vertical planks, serves to heighten the effect of the building floating skyward as the viewer's eye is led upward from the board-and-batten siding to the vergeboards, meeting at the apex of the Gothic arch, where a crowning finial frequently completes the trip to the clouds.

Aspiration is the message, and the skyward-soaring Gothic arches say it beautifully. In contrast to the earlier Greek Revival form, a classical box-style house with predictable columns, Gothic Revival offers variations in shape, decorative detail, and the thrill of multiple triangular lines. Some have the spires and battlements of medieval Gothic castles, reminiscent of the fantasy world of knights and dragons.

This was the first of the Victorian styles to reach America.

❧ W h e r e : **Predominantly New England, where the movement began and flourished; rare in the South and on the West Coast.**

❧ W h e n : **1840–1880**

❧ L o o k   f o r :

> *Steeply pitched roofs*
> *Vergeboard (or bargeboard) trim along roof edges*
> *Pointed-arch, high dormer windows*
> *Pointed Gothic windows: lancets and other shapes*
> *Board-and-batten siding*

A wide Gothic arch decorated with ivory scallop trim joins the porch supports.

Facing page: This High Gothic Revival villa has fancy vergeboards on every gable edge. Windows come in various shapes, many with pointed eyebrows. It is the multistyled tower and the building's sheer mass that earn it the villa title. The tower is the centerpiece of this bed-and-breakfast inn in Cape May, New Jersey.

*F*ar left: Shadows of the vergeboards along the edges of the roof gable change as the sun moves. The red-tipped finial at the gable apex is repeated on every major gable. The dark-green belt course of pierced board over a light-colored board and the wave pattern of the shingles are embellishments borrowed from the Queen Anne style.

*L*eft: This trio of pointed Gothic windows has red mullions bursting into tracery at the tops. A shelf projection between the top and bottom windows gives the suggestion of a balcony and is decorated with red-tipped Italianate brackets underneath.

A sycamore tree frames this view of the tower, featuring a mansard roof and a Gothic gable with finial. Note the vergeboard trim on the arch above the stained-glass roundel window. The lacy ironwork at the top of the roof is called cresting, and is a Second Empire design.

bove left: The trefoil window, beneath the gable, is outlined in brown, and its curves are reiterated in flowing vergeboards above it. Note the carved-leaf design at the vergeboards apex and the brown-tipped pendant. *Above center:* Pointed latticed windows share an eyebrow protection at their top. *Above right:* The four-petaled clover, or quatrefoil, and the dagger pointing away from the clover are favorite Gothic Revival shapes. Above them is a balustrade of medieval-inspired design.

This Gothic Revival cottage is built of rusticated wood, scored to look like stone blocks. Brown quoins along the edges complete the resemblance to masonry.

Above: A side view of this many-gabled, board-and-batten cottage shows off the projecting oriel window, directly below a large pointed finial and pendant. Below the oriel is an immense window of vertical glass panels arching into tracery.

Above right: The brown vergeboards and finials in the trio of Gothic gables complement the light-rose color of the siding. A bay window on the first floor has wooden cresting that matches the cresting on the portico above the entrance.

Right: Shadows from the vergeboards and the pendant present unsuspected shapes on the board-and-batten siding.

Twin parapeted gables adorn this rambling Gothic Revival cottage. Dark-green balls top the finials on every parapet. The double-stack chimneys with chimney pots are a Gothic feature. The veranda is taken from the Queen Anne Free Classic style.

Left and below: This asymmetrically shaped house has both board-and-batten and horizontal siding. Its elaborately trimmed gable and dormer windows are accented by the use of stark white paint. Unusual gable trusses end as dropped pendants and are intersected by knobbed crossboards.

Facing page: The elaborate trim work on this board-and-batten sided cottage is emphasized by its dusty-plum color. The flared pagoda-styled gable and wave-patterned vergeboard is crowned by an elongated finial with pendant. Note the chimney fretwork.

This house in Maine has a tall center gable, emphasizing the cathedral look of the stained-glass window above the porch balcony. The rusticated wood siding is painted an authentic Victorian beige color. The porch support (*shown in detail on the facing page*) echoes the scrollwork of the vergeboards but with an elongated Gothic arch.

The medieval-style latticed lancet window with a Y-tracery design points to a round heraldic patera above. The shadows cast by the vergeboards create an illusion of un-dulating spikes.

Two massive ornamental chimneys with terra-cotta chimney pots flank the center gable. Built in 1846, the William Rotch house in New Bedford, Massachusetts, was designed by A. J. Davis.

The porch support repeats the latticework in the windows.

The three-sided oriel window features white castellated trim on top and six slender lancets.

Facing page: Intricate white vergeboards with a fleur-de-lis pattern and a massive pendant point to the decorative white balcony and lancet window.

A Victorian mix, this amazing, lacy concoction is actually a Federal-style house remodeled into Gothic Revival excess. Spires of white froth reach skyward above the castellated roof with an uncharacteristic railing and balusters.

The Pickering house in Salem, Massachusetts, was built in 1651, then remodeled into this Gothic Revival twin-gabled cottage.

The illusion of height is accentuated by the use of board-and-batten siding, an elongated gable, and narrow windows stacked one above the other.

ITALIANATE

The gay and sunny temperament of the South of Europe is well expressed in the light balconies, the grouped windows, the open arcades and the statue and vase bordered terraces of the Venetian and Italian villas. . . .

—A. J. Downing, *The Architecture of Country Houses*, 1850

A low-pitched or low-hipped roof with large supportive decorative brackets is the outstanding feature of Italianates. In fact, the style was sometimes called "the bracketed mode." It can be easily recognized by its bold square or rectangular shape which, it has been said, symbolizes security, strength, and integrity.

Imitations of the typical Northern Italian farmhouse architecture were featured in Andrew Jackson Downing's books, which also popularized Gothic Revival architecture. Italianate progressed from an early simple form to what has been called High Italianate. Fanciful embellishments were added: square towers, cupolas of all shapes, windows with curved decorative crowns, and large cornice brackets. Occasionally, small entry porches were added. For the first time, large, heavy glass panels were used in doors. The more elaborate towered styles are labeled Italianate Villas.

The popularity of Italianates faded shortly after the depression of the 1870s together with the concurrently popular Second Empires, and were replaced by Queen Annes in the latter part of that decade.

Where: Most common in the Midwest, Northern California, and some cities of the Northeast. Relatively rare in the South.

When: 1840–1885

Look for:

Low-pitched or low-hipped roof, flat in appearance
Large supporting brackets under eaves
Square or rectangular towers
Cupolas
Windows with hoods or eyebrows

A*bove:* A frequent Italianate adornment is the cupola, shown here in three varieties from plain to fancy.

F*acing page:* A Rhode Island Italianate villa features bracketed roof lines and a tower with dormer windows and cupola. Under the left gable is an Italian loggia with rounded arches.

Now a fully restored bed-and-breakfast inn in Cape May, New Jersey, this inviting yellow Italianate was built as Jackson's gambling club in 1872. The primary feature of this bracketed Italianate is its large veranda with double-columned, Venetian entry supports, which have a spiral design. The yellow cupola on the roof and the tall, long windows on the first floor are other typical Italianate features. Such windows and high ceilings are commonly used to help cool rooms in hot weather.

Facing page: The Victorian forerunner to television, a stereoscope viewer, lies on the small marble-top table in the foreground next to a rose-colored Victorian chaperone chair, or tête-à-tête. The striking wall and ceiling paper is available today.

A hand-silk-screened wallpaper border decorates this bedroom featuring Renaissance Revival furniture. A chandelier hanging from the ceiling is black-lacquered brass.

This Italianate exhibits classical columns and a bracketed, low-pitched roof with a pediment over its entrance.

Pedimented windows with dentils along the brackets distinguish this Napa, California, Italianate.

Facing page: This towered beige-and-white Italianate sporting Stick-style embellishments and a few Gothic finials stands on a San Francisco hillside. Note its columned portico with a balustrade.

This Italianate has French Revival embellishments: lacework balconies and elaborate windows. The rusticated-wood wall resembles masonry. The sculptural embellishment (*below*) together with the dentils behind it function as a balcony corbel.

Above: A classic gray-and-white double-bayed Italianate house in San Francisco has been enlivened with blue trim accents.

Above right: This Eureka, California, mixed Victorian with a false gable front, rectangular bay, corner boards, and belt course has elements of Stick, Italianate, and Queen Anne.

Right: The small scale of the tiny pale-yellow bracketed Italianate (*on the right*) with a bay window is a California phenomenon. Next door, the Queen Anne has black, white and gold trim.

SECOND EMPIRE

All architecture is what you do to it when you look upon it.

—Walt Whitman

Second Empire's distinguishing feature is the mansard roof. Designed to have a double slope on all four sides, the roof's second and steep slope comes in concave, convex, straight, and S-curve designs. Practical as well as handsome, mansard roofs permit a top floor of fully usable room space, compared to the cramped attics of gabled roof lines. Second Empire houses are square or rectangular, occasionally towered, and often decorated in the Italianate manner, causing a casual observer some confusion. The overhang and brackets are usually smaller than those of an Italianate house.

Muted red, green, blue, or tan patterns were often created by placement of roof tiles on Second Empire roof slopes. Ironwork cresting frequently graced some of the house tops. Varying window types—paired, pedimented, and round-arched—add interest to the façade. Quoins and a belt course of contrasting colors are other Second Empire ornamental devices.

The French flavor in Victorian architecture is seen in the mansard roof, which derives its name from François Mansart, a seventeenth-century architect. The mansard roof, a mid-century hit at exhibitions in Paris, moved on to England and then to America.

❧ Where : Frequent in Northeast and Midwest. Comparatively rare on the West Coast or in the South.

❧ When : 1855–1885

❧ Look for :

Mansard roofs
Square or rectangular shape, occasionally with a tower
Colored-tile patterns and ironwork cresting on roofs
Belt courses and quoins in contrasting colors

Built in 1882, this Second Empire house has a polychromed mansard roof with three dormer windows. The pediment on the dormer window (*shown on facing page*) includes a truss with pendant and scrollwork finial, reminiscent of the Gothic Revival style.

M ore features of this house include two symmetrical bays and a two-story front porch, which has been extended on the first floor.

R oof brackets of the Second Empire style are finer and smaller than Italianate brackets, with less roof overhang. Note the cutout designs of the fascia board.

The colored-tile pattern on this mansard roof is topped with a cupola. A dark-green-and-cream-colored frieze encircles the house just below the cornice.

A double door with glass panels, a frequent Second Empire feature, has vertical strips of fish-scale shingles on the door trim and diamond-shaped appliqués on each of the curved brackets that support the portico. Sensuous ball pendants hang from the bracket tips. Colors are from the authentic paint palette of the era.

The distinctive red mansard roof of this house sits atop gray-green matching bays and a centered entry. The house is painted in authentic mid-Victorian colors.

This Second Empire structure is fashionably attended by a rear carriage house. Both buildings are set off with cupolas and white quoins. The second-story modified Palladian window is repeated on a smaller scale in the center dormer window on the roof.

The hexagonal cupola encircled by dentils is topped by a heavy post finial.

Facing page: The rich colors and tones of wood, wallpaper, and rugs in this dining room and hall exemplify the opulence of Victorian decor.

An otherwise simple Second Empire house has been enlivened by cream, red, and dark-green paint, highlighting the extensive ornamental trim. Iron roof cresting completes the fancy dress of this dwelling.

At the handsome oak double door, square cream-colored panels with dark-green paterae decorate the porch ceiling and the underside of the window overhang. Painting also accentuates the details on the portico and bay window.

Finely carved, Renaissance-style walnut woodwork of the Château-sur-Mer library was designed by a Florentine decorator and delivered, assembled, and installed in Newport, Rhode Island, in 1876.

If there is a High Octagon, this is it. The immense baroque-domed roof with cupola and elongated finial gives the Armour-Steiner house in Irvington-on-Hudson, New York, an imposing grandness. The large paired and pedimented double windows in the dome are punctuated by round window projections. The wraparound porch, which is typical of this style, has paired porch supports and a lacy Queen Anne balustrade.

OCTAGON

But is the square form the best of all? Is the right-angle the best angle? Can not some radical improvement be made, both in the outside form and the internal arrangement of our houses? Nature's forms are mostly SPHERICAL. She makes ten thousand curvilineal to one square figure. Then why not apply her forms to house? Fruits, eggs, tubers, nuts, grains, seeds, trees, etc., are made spherical, in order to inclose the most material in the least compass. Since, as already shown, a circle incloses more space for its surface than any other form, of course the nearer spherical our houses, the more inside room for the outside wall, besides being more comfortable. . . . Of course the octagon, by approximating the circle, incloses more space for its wall than the square, besides being more compact and available.

—Orson S. Fowler, *The Octagon House: A Home for All*, rev. ed., 1853

Of all the Victorian styles, the Octagon is the simplest to identify with its eight-sided construction. Some adaptations have six, ten, or more sides. Many sport octagonal cupolas or domes and porches; most have a raised basement. There are plain as well as decorated models, the latter carrying Gothic, Italianate, and sometimes Greek Revival embellishments.

The Octagon house was said to be closest to nature's own form, the sphere. The rounded shape allows for more usable interior living space, claimed Orson Fowler in his book *The Octagon House: A Home for All*. He said that the eight-sided house could provide more sunlight, heat, ventilation, and better communication between rooms, eliminating dark corners. A self-styled humanitarian, he designed dwellings "within reach of the poorer classes." Revolutionary and advanced in his thinking, Fowler advocated extensive use of glass as nature's roofing and flooring materials. He was adamant that water closets be located inside the home as a necessity for the family, and he supported the use of hot-air furnaces and other period inventions.

His highly successful book was quoted by nearly every leading Victorian pattern book and had impact in England, France, and China. His do-it-yourself techniques were a delight to every man building his own home. Fowler built his monstrous sixty-room Octagon home in 1853. But the Octagon house, along with the eccentric Fowler, began to decline with the Panic of 1857.

Where: A rare style (only a few hundred remain), scattered in New York, New England, the Midwest, and the West Coast.

When: 1850–1870

Look for:

Eight-sided (more or less)
Low-pitched, hipped roofs
Raised basements
Roof cupolas

R estoration work is evident on one of the last great Octagons remaining in this country. Its private owner is fighting valiantly to maintain this endangered species as federal grants disappear.

W hite quoins highlight this blue-gray Octagon house in San Francisco. Built in 1857, it has an octagonal cupola on its low-hipped roof. It is one of only two remaining Octagons in the city.

A severe and simple Octagon house is this working man's model with a dormer window. A small solid portico decorates the entrance, and hoods over windows deflect rain and snow.

F *acing page:* In one of the first uses of American Indian textile patterns, these handsome geometric designs stencilled in silver on red walls and ceiling are reported to have been designed by Louis B. Tiffany for the Mark Twain house in Hartford, Connecticut. Startling Eastlake patterns evolve on each level of the stairwell. Note the elaborate ironwork gas lamp on the stair newel post.

EXOTIC REVIVAL

So there remains in the art of architecture something that evades analysis, something that touches us in the most secret parts of our minds, something not only beyond utility but also beyond all that is rational and everyday. It could not be otherwise for our biggest, toughest, most complex, most permanent, and most powerful art.

—Stanley Abercrombie, *Architecture as Art*, 1984

Architectural elements from faraway or "exotic" places were creatively adapted to basic Victorian structures. Called Exotic Revival, this classification includes Oriental, Swiss Chalet, and Egyptian.

Oriental Exotic features onion-shaped or Turkish domes, usually on an Italianate house, sometimes with added oriental trim. Inspired by trade with China and India, this style, although rare, was a long-lived one, lasting the full half-century.

Swiss Chalet is instantly recognizable by an excess of carpenter's lace, or gingerbread, on sec-ond-story porches. Chalets often have a low-pitched front-gabled roof. In some cases, it is obvious that the trim and the full-front balcony have been added to an already existing structure. A. J. Downing is responsible for bringing the contemporary chalet to America through his book *The Architecture of Country Houses.*

Egyptian Exotic Revival is quite rare and what survives is mostly in public buildings. Of masonry rather than wood, the style featured papyrus-like leaf columns on Italianate-style buildings.

Where: Rare throughout the United States. Swiss Chalet is often found in Eastern seaside resorts.

When: 1835–1890

Left: Sunlight creates an art object of a nest of sensual, spired onion domes, encircling one large mother dome.

Facing page: This massive San Francisco building has a wraparound balcony with scalloped arch supports and convex-shaped balusters, which create a Moorish feeling. Note the intricate brackets under the balcony overhang.

Left: This view of the Vedanta Society headquarters shows an array of oriental embellishments from the onion dome to mosquelike arches complete with a castellated Victorian tower. A French heraldic symbol is appliquéd to the siding.

Left: Second-floor porches have a frivolous gingerbread trim in this Connecticut Swiss chalet, with vinelike designs framed at the top of the porch supports.

An array of Swiss Chalet vacation homes line this street in Ocean Grove, New Jersey.

Balustrade designs and sunbursts add a fireworks effect to this three-story Swiss Chalet with sawtooth vergeboards.

STICK

The strength and character of the style depends almost wholly on the shadows which are thrown upon its surface by projecting members.

—Henry W. Cleaveland, *Village and Farm Cottages*, 1856

Decorative stickwork—horizontal, vertical, and diagonal boards placed on top of wooden clapboard or shingles—is the outstanding feature of this style house and repeats the inner structural framework on the exterior of the house and lends an almost pre-Tudor look to the structure.

Roofs are gabled and often steeply pitched with cross gables. Look for decorative braces, sticklike brackets, knee braces, stick pendants, dormers, gables with embellished trusses, wide overhang of eaves, and exposed rafter ends. Some houses have a square or rectangular tower. One-story porches have Y-shaped sticklike supports.

Because the Stick style expressed the inner-frame construction, it is said to have structural honesty. A growth from Gothic Revival and a bridge to the Queen Anne house, the style was popularized by pattern books similar to, but more detailed than, Andrew Jackson Downing's. Some consider the Stick style High Victorian Gothic.

  Where : **Primarily in the Northeast and the Northwest.**

  When :   **1860–1890**

  Look for :

> *Small vertical, horizontal, or diagonal planks placed on top of exterior walls*
> *Steeply gabled roofs with decorative chimneys*
> *Embellished trusses and sticklike brackets*
> *Y-shaped porch supports*

This Stick-style cottage features deep-red timbered gables over a large center balcony and porch. Spindle balusters (*shown on facing page*) decorate the balcony and are repeated on the veranda pediment. Heavier balustrade posts of red end in ball pendants.

49

An irregular roof with dormers and gables graces this Stick-style Cape May cottage, now a house museum. The yellow Y-shaped porch supports and clapboard siding are decorated with dark-green beams. Capped decorative brick chimneys are a Stick feature. The red scalloped roof tiles complement the cream-and-dark-green hooded dormer windows. Dark-green exterior beams outline the form of the house and are decorated with multiple pierced circular holes. The vertical stick patterns and brackets appear to support the overhanging gable. The pierced-circle theme is repeated in these appendages.

Geometric blue-and-gold wallpaper lightens the library of the Mark Twain house in Hartford, Connecticut. The enormous, intricately carved wooden mantel was brought by Twain from a castle in Scotland. The wooden arched doorway leads to the glass-walled conservatory.

An eclectic Stick-style Queen Anne in Hartford, Connecticut, features a two-story windowed bay and a trussed gable and portico pediment. The red-and-dark-green belt course matches third-floor body colors.

Two nearly identical Stick-style houses in New Haven, Connecticut, show how color treatment can vary the appearance of the façade. The yellow house with gray beams has a timbered gable and pedimented entry. The blue-gray version has the same timbered gable, less noticeable in white beams on gray. Both houses have decorative brick chimneys. *Right:* The spindle-spoked arch casts intriguing shadows on the wall of this second-floor balcony.

Vertical and horizontal beams highlight the framework of this Stick-style Queen Anne. Sawtooth shingles decorate the porch pediment and front gable.

Wooden mantel posts were designed with other interior woodwork by the architect Frank Furness. A floral plaster frieze encircles the room at ceiling height and was an 1890 addition, along with the scroll design on the ceiling.

The skeleton effect of Stick-style framing is evident in the Griswold house at Newport, Rhode Island. Note the multicolored tile patterns on the roof and the wide veranda with Y-beam supports. The house was the first Newport commission of architect Richard Morris Hunt.

Bays everywhere, gabled in all directions, towered, balconied, and bracketed, this eclectic Queen Anne house was completed by a California lumber baron in 1886. A magnificent wraparound porch has columns elaborately decorated with heavy balls and rings. Finials abound on each roof cap or gable.

QUEEN ANNE

Proportion in architecture has been aptly likened to time in music—the measure which confers a completeness of form on the entire melody.

—A. J. Downing

The culmination of all other Victorian styles, the Queen Anne displays the entire panorama of Victorian decorations. These houses are the most provocative, seductive, brazen, tongue-in-cheek architecture ever produced by man. The Queen Anne style has a multifaceted house shape presenting arrangements of every conceivable form of wall alteration. Textured wall surfaces, displaying various shapes of shingles, are common.

Roofs may have finials, vergeboards, brackets under trim or gables, cresting, tall chimneys with carvings or terra-cotta panels, as well as domed turrets. Windows can be stained glass and of varying shapes and designs. Overhanging second stories, circular or square bays, cantilevered wall extensions, verandas, and wraparound porches all break up frontal space.

The sheer exuberance of it all can astound, amuse, and fascinate the delighted observer—or offend those who prefer their landscapes simple and clean.

Like a beautiful woman, a Queen Anne house changes its shape and allure as the light changes by season or time of day.

To further identify Queen Anne cottages, substyles have been suggested by *A Field Guide to American Houses*. The most popular is Spindlework, known for its gingerbread decoration. Beadwork, knobs, delicate porch supports, and lace-like carpentry work are frequent. Raised designs featuring the sun, the moon, or floral patterns, called Eastlake ornamentation, are sometimes found on Spindlework houses.

Free Classic Queen Anne houses feature porches with sturdy Greek or Roman columns as supports. Palladian windows, dentils along the cornice, and pedimented porch entrances without trim are some exterior additions to this style.

English architects borrowed from the earlier Elizabethan and Jacobean eras to produce the Queen Anne style. American adaptations were many, and it was the most popular of all Victorian dwellings.

⋟ **Where :** Most frequently in the West and the South. Examples in the Northeast are less common except at seaside resorts.

⋟ **When :** 1880–1910

⋟ **Look for :**

Irregular house shapes

Multiple projections from walls, including bay windows, towers, turrets, porches, and balconies

Decorative trim, including patterned shingles, brackets, belt courses

Yellow fish-scale shingles are the field for a stylized sunburst.

An Italianate tower adorns this Queen Anne Spindlework dwelling. Eastlake-style vergeboards decorate the gables.

This massive Spindlework Queen Anne residence has a hipped roof with slightly lower cross gables and a gabled, pedimented entry. Decorative brickwork on the side-wall chimney (*right*) is further enhanced with a terra-cotta swag motif. Notice the panelled belt course.

The intricately carved details (*below*) are only two of many on this house. A sunflower-carved bracket is on a second-floor cutaway window, and Bacchus with open mouth, wreathed in a grape-and-vine design, is under spindlework on the balcony.

Two layers of spindlework with spiral porch columns decorate the front entrance.

W hite and black trim dresses this small gray Queen Anne and emphasizes the beauty of symmetry in its ornate embellishments.

T his turreted balcony with a witch's cap is decorated with brightly painted turned posts and trim details. The same colors are repeated in the gingerbread trim on the rest of the house.

An electrified gasolier hangs over the large 1860 Renaissance Revival dining-room table that seats twelve. At the left, the massive walnut sideboard with carved wolf's head at its top has lighter chestnut wood carvings and a Tennessee marble top. The gold-and-green hand-stencilled wallpaper and the elaborate window treatments complete this room, which exemplifies the grand scale of Victorian furnishings.

These two unusually carved, multicolored gable embellishments are found in Newport, Rhode Island.

Facing page and right: The paint combinations on this Northern California house highlight identical frieze borders around its base, middle, and top. The semicircular horseshoe arches hung from the entrance and cutaway bay windows give it a Moorish feeling.

Two balconied towers with witch's caps decorate this Newport, Rhode Island, house. Note a wide golden-yellow horizontal border under the front gable.

This eclectic cottage is primarily Queen Anne, but with strong overtones of Gothic Revival. The roof lines, towered bays, and first-floor window pediments are Queen Anne forms, while the vergeboards, trusses, finials, and arch are Gothic Revival features.

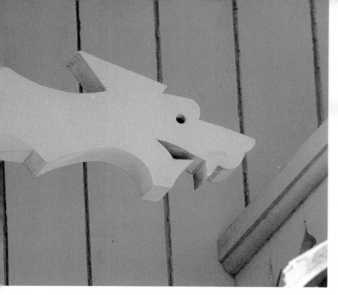

Much of the charm of this Rhode Island cottage is derived from its intricate sawed trim work. A most unusual feature is the red-and-white hexagonal-shaped tile band around the first floor.

Facing page: Direct sunlight casts shadows from the multifaceted carving and shingles, that adorn this Queen Anne house. A variety of sunburst designs decorate the pedimented porch and dormer behind it. Fish-scale shingles finish the gable apex. *At right:* Multiple shingle patterns of crenellated and pointed sawtooth shapes surround a carved rectangular panel.

The onion-shaped tower cap gives a Moorish flavor to this Spindlework Queen Anne with a large veranda.

Above: The horseshoe arch on the balcony has a crenellated shingle design behind it. Note the elaborately decorated brackets with pendants (*shown right*).

An onion dome with French Revival swag appliqué encircling it is the crowning feature of this Queen Anne house.

Intricate geometric designs are emphasized by contrasting colors.

Overleaf: A hillside of Queen Anne houses in San Francisco illustrates the variety of forms in the style.

Two entrances, one pedimented, are part of the charm of this gabled Queen Anne. White trim on the posts and columns give a heavy vertical accent to the house.

This one-story Italianate–Queen Anne in Northern California features Eastlake designs on its pedimented bay fronts.

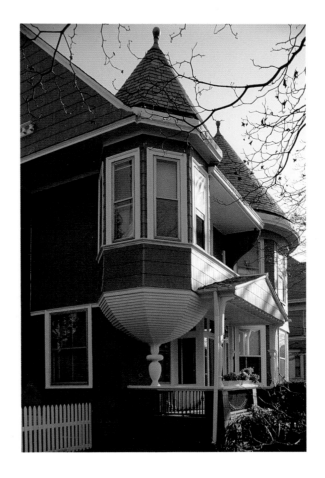

bove: This Free Classic Queen Anne features a Moorish or horseshoe design vergeboard on the gable above an Eastlake-ornamented pediment.

ight: This corbeled bay has a white support post attached to the porch balustrade.

In this Cape May, New Jersey, house, the surrounding porch with intricately painted spindlework is topped by a tower.

A large, central five-sided tower front with a cupola is the entry to this side-gabled Queen Anne.

This Free Classic style features round porches under a squat, conical tower.

The small blue beam extensions under the pediment and the gable eaves are a Stick-style feature. The orange semicircular fan above the paired windows is an Eastlake decoration. Rainbow coloration on the pediment is a West Coast adaptation.

An original solid brass chandelier, made by Cornelius and Baker of Philadelphia, hangs over the walnut Renaissance Revival dining table, also an original furnishing in the Mainstay Inn at Cape May, New Jersey. The wide wall frieze visually lowers the fourteen-foot ceiling.

The slender Queen Anne town house on the left boasts a black witch's cap and latticework on the second-floor balcony. Next door, a front-gabled Free Classic Queen Anne is startling with its black-and-white ornamentation.

Carved and painted Eastlake decorations of shell, sunflower, and scroll adorn this opulently detailed California country house. Spindlework at left features a third-floor balcony with decorated vergeboard, pendant, Eastlake balusters, and trim.

This small Queen Anne–Italianate cottage is one of many that dot the hills of San Francisco. Note the roof pediment over the paired windows and the trussed porch pediment.

This massive, rambling Shingle cottage has multiple roof lines and a large porch with squat, shingled tower, elements typical of its style.

Even the porch columns are shingled on this seaside resort house.

SHINGLE

He who loves an old house
Never Loves in vain
How can an old house
Used to sun and rain,
To Lilac and larkspur,
And an elm above,
Ever fail to answer
The heart that gives it love?

—Isabel Fiske Conant, 1903

Exteriors covered in shingles earmark these Victorian structures, which have little or no ornamentation. Massive in size, Shingle houses have a variety of roof lines: gambrel, front-gabled, side-gabled, cross-gabled, and hipped with cross gables.

Often, large roomy porches with simple classic columns extend partially around the two- or three-storied house. Some are built of masonry on the first floor and shingled above that. Others flaunt towers, bays, multiple windows, and heavy, wide arches.

The color of most Shingle-style houses is either dark brown or white. Shingle houses are now using newly applied cedar shake shingles, which mellow into a natural silver-gray finish.

The last of the Victorian styles, it is considered to be an original American style. Shingle evolved into the smaller shingle-covered bungalow.

Where: Originating in New England, this style is found throughout the country.

When: 1880–1900

Look for:

Shingles everywhere
Lack of decoration, no corner boards
Variety of roof lines
Large porches

Fresh shingles and blue shutters brighten an original Shingle house in Cape May, New Jersey.

GLOSSARY

Acroterion—a pedestal or design on the ends or apex of a pediment.

Baluster—a small, upright spindle or post, which, when used in a series, supports a handrail.

Balustrade—the entire railing system, which includes a handrail on top of a row of balusters and sometimes a bottom rail.

Bay—a structural protrusion, which often contains windows.

Bay window—a window or windows in a wall that projects outward.

Belt course—a horizontal band around a building, usually with a molding.

Bracket—a support that projects from a wall, sometimes in the shape of an inverted L.

Cantilever—an unsupported beam or other member that projects beyond its supporting wall, sometimes under a cornice or eaves of a house.

Carpenter's lace—see **Gingerbread**.

Corbel—a form, usually created by extending successive layers of masonry or wood beyond the wall surface.

Corner board—a board trim on the exterior corner of wood frame houses.

Cornice—any molded projection at the top of a wall that crowns or finishes it.

Crenellated—a pattern of repeated alternate depressions; having battlements.

Cresting—a decorative ridge on a roof; a continuous rhythmic series of finials, often in ironwork.

Cupola—a small rooftop structure, round or many-sided, with its own roof.

Dentil—one of a band of small, square toothlike blocks that form a molding.

Dormer—a projection from the roof that increases space inside and usually has a window on the gable end.

Eastlake—exterior house decorations of a light geometric style, as well as scroll and floral appliqués on walls; named for furniture designer Charles Eastlake.

Eyebrow—molding over the top of a window or door; sometimes called a *hood*.

Fascia—a horizontal band, sometimes used in combination with narrow moldings.

Finial—an ornament at the top of a gable, pinnacle, spire, or other high point.

Fretwork—ornamental openwork or intersecting bars in relief, usually minute and elaborate, in contrasting colors.

Frieze—a decorative band on a wall.

Gable—the upper triangular section of an end wall under a pitched roof.

Gambrel roof—features two roof slopes on each side, the lower being the longer and steeper of the two.

Gasolier—a chandelier that uses gas.

Gingerbread—rich decorations on American Victorian buildings, also called *carpenter's lace*.

Hood—see **Eyebrow**.

Lancet window—a narrow, tall, sharply pointed window.

Lattice—openwork grill of crossed interlocking strips.

Loggia—an arcaded or colonnaded passage, open on one or both sides.

Mansard roof—sloped on all four sides in two planes, the lower of which is concave, convex, straight-lined, or S-shaped.

Mullion—the vertical dividing member between windows, windowpanes, or doors.

Newel post—the bottom, larger post of a staircase balustrade.

Oriel window—a bay window that is corbeled out from the wall of an upper story.

Palladian—an arched opening closely flanked by openings of smaller size and with the same base; named for Andrea Palladio, the Italian architect.

Parapet—a low wall at the edge of a roof, balcony, terrace, battlement, etc.

Patera—a flat round or oval medallion, often used to ornament friezes.

Pediment—the triangular front on a roof gable; sometimes over windows or doors.

Polychromed—decorated in a variety of colors.

Portico—an entrance porch that has a roof supported by columns or brackets.

Quatrefoil—a four-lobed design.

Quoins—cornerstones of a wall.

Roundel—a small circular window or panel; small bead molding.

Rusticated wood—wood incised in block shapes to resemble stone.

Spindlework—a Queen Anne decoration featuring short, turned parts, similar to balusters.

Tracery—curving mullions of a Gothic Revival window.

Trefoil—a three-lobed clover pattern.

Truss—a triangular structure, usually straight-sided, that creates a rigid framework.

Turret—a small tower, often corbeled, at corner of building.

Vergeboard—an ornamental decorated board hanging from a gable roof edge (also called *bargeboard*).

Witch's cap—a conical roof on a tower.

SUGGESTED READINGS

Victorian House Architecture and Interiors

Andrews, Wayne. *American Gothic: Its Origins, Its Trials, Its Triumphs.* New York: Random House, 1975.

Barber, George F. *Cottage Souvenir, Number Two.* 1890. Reprint. Watkins Glen, N.Y.: American Life Foundation, 1982.

Berg, Donald J. *Country Patterns, 1841–1883: A Sampler of Nineteenth-Century Rural Homes and Gardens.* New York: Antiquity Reprints, 1982.

Clark, Kenneth. *The Gothic Revival: An Essay in the History of Taste.* New York: Harper & Row, 1962.

Dixon, Roger, and Stefan Muthesius. *Victorian Architecture.* New York: Oxford University Press, 1978.

Downing, Andrew Jackson. *The Architecture of Country Houses.* 1850. Reprint. New York: Dover Publications, 1969.

———. *Victorian Cottage Residences.* 5th ed. 1873. Reprint. New York: Dover Publications, 1981.

Fowler, Orson S. *The Octagon House: A Home for All.* Rev. ed., 1853. Reprint. New York: Dover Publications, 1973.

Gillon, Edmund V., Jr., and Clay Lancaster. *Victorian Houses: A Treasury of Lesser-Known Examples.* New York: Dover Publications, 1973.

Grow, Lawrence, and Dina Von Zweck. *American Victorian: A Style and Sourcebook.* New York: Harper & Row, 1984.

Hitchcock, Henry Russell. *The Architecture of H. H. Richardson and His Times.* Cambridge: MIT Press, 1981.

Hussey, E. C. *Victorian Home Building: A Transcontinental View of 1875.* Reprint. Watkins Glen, N.Y.: American Life Foundation, 1976.

Karp, Ben. *Ornamental Carpentry on Nineteenth-Century American Houses.* New York: Dover Publications, 1981.

Lewis, Arnold. *American Country Houses of the Gilded Age.* 1886–87. Reprint of *Sheldon's Artistic Country Seats.* New York: Dover Publications, 1982.

Maas, John. *The Gingerbread Age: A View of Victorian America.* New York: Greenwich House, 1983.

McArdle, Alma, and Deirdre McArdle. *Carpenter Gothic: Nineteenth-Century Ornamented Houses of New England.* New York: Whitney Library of Design, 1983.

Mitchell, Eugene. *American Victoriana.* New York: Van Nostrand Reinhold, 1983.

Morgan, Keith, ed. *American Victorian Architecture.* 1886. Reprint of *L'Architecture Américaine.* New York: Dover Publications, 1975.

Moss, Roger. *Century of Color: Exterior Decoration for American Buildings 1820–1920.* Watkins Glen, N.Y.: American Life Foundation, 1981. (Available from The Athenaeum Museum, 219 So. Sixth St., Philadelphia, Pa. 19106.)

Olwell, Carol, and Judith Lynch Waldham. *A Gift to the Street: A Celebration of Victorian Architecture.* New York: St. Martin's Press, 1976.

Palliser, George, and Charles Palliser. *The Palliser's Late Victorian Architecture.* 1888. Reprint of *American Architecture.* Watkins Glen, N.Y.: American Life Foundation, 1978.

Pomada, Elizabeth, and Michael Larsen. *Painted Ladies: San Francisco's Resplendent Victorians.* New York: E. P. Dutton, 1978.

Rosenberg, John D., ed. *The Genius of John Ruskin, Selections from His Writings.* New York: Vail Ballou Press, 1979.

Ruskin, John. *The Seven Lamps of Architecture.* 1849. Reprint. New York: Farrar, Straus & Giroux, 1979.

———. *The Stones of Venice.* 1851. Reprint edited by Jan Morris. Boston: Little, Brown & Co., 1981.

Scully, Vincent J., Jr. *The Shingle Style and the Stick Style.* Rev. ed. New Haven, Conn.: Yale University Press, 1955.

Seale, William. *The Tasteful Interlude: American Interiors Through the Camera's Eye, 1860–1917.* 2nd ed. Nashville, Tenn.: American Association for State and Local History, 1981.

Shoppell, R. W. *Turn-of-the-Century Houses, Cottages and Villas, Floor Plans and Line Illustrations.* 1890. Reprint. New York: Dover Publications, 1983.

Sloan, Samuel. *Sloan's Victorian Buildings.* 1852. Reprint of *The Model Architect.* New York: Dover Publications, 1980.

Steegman, John. *Victorian Taste: A Study of the Arts and Architecture from 1830 to 1870.* Cambridge: MIT Press, 1971.

Swedburg, Robert, and Harriet Swedburg. *Victorian Furniture, Book II, Styles and Prices.* Rev. ed. New York: Wallace-Homestead, 1983.

Vaux, Calvert. *Villas and Cottages: The Great Architectural Style Book of the Hudson River School.* 1864. Reprint. New York: Dover Publications, 1970.

General Architectural Information

Abercrombie, Stanley. *Architecture as Art: An Esthetic Analysis*. New York: Van Nostrand Reinhold, 1984.

Abramovitz, Anita. *People and Spaces: A View of History Through Architecture*. New York: The Viking Press, 1979.

Blumenson, John J. G. *Identifying American Architecture*. 2nd ed. Nashville, Tenn.: American Association for State and Local History, 1981.

Foley, Mary Mix. *The American House*. New York: Harper & Row, 1980.

Grillo, Paul Jacques. *Form, Function and Design*. New York: Dover Publications, 1960.

Haneman, John Theodore. *Pictorial Encyclopedia of Historical Architectural Plans, Details and Elements*. 1923. Reprint. New York: Dover Publications, 1984.

Harris, Cyril M. *Illustrated Dictionary of Historic Architecture*. New York: Dover Publications, 1977.

Hunt, William Dudley, Jr. *American Architecture*. New York: Harper & Row, 1984.

McAlester, Virginia, and Lee McAlester. *A Field Guide to American Houses*. New York: Alfred A. Knopf, 1984.

Pevsner, Nikolaus, John Fleming, and Hugh Honour. *A Dictionary of Architecture*. Woodstock, N.Y.: Overlook Press, 1976.

Poppeliers, John C., S. Allen Chambers, and Nancy B. Schwartz. *What Style Is It?* Washington, D.C.: Preservation Press, 1983.

Rifkind, Carole. *A Field Guide to American Architecture*. New York: New American Library, 1980.

Saylor, Henry H. *Dictionary of Architecture*. New York: John Wiley & Sons, 1952.

Ware, Dora, and Maureen Stafford. *An Illustrated Dictionary of Ornament*. New York: St. Martin's Press, 1974.

Wrenn, Tony, and Elizabeth D. Mulloy. *America's Forgotten Architecture*. New York: Pantheon Books, 1976.

Restoration and Preservation Guidance

Labine, Clem, ed. *The Old House Journal Compendium*. Woodstock, N.Y.: Overlook Press, 1980.

Maddox, Diane, ed. *The Brown Book: A Directory of Preservation Information*. Washington, D.C.: Preservation Press, 1983.

National Trust for Historic Preservation. *Directory of Private, Nonprofit Preservation Organizations: State and Local Levels*. Washington, D.C.: Preservation Press, 1980.

Vila, Bob. *This Old House*. New York: E. P. Dutton, 1981.

DIRECTORY OF ADDRESSES

The grand finale of *Victorious Victorians* was on the West Coast at Eureka, California, where (*from left*) photographer Taylor Lewis, author Peg Sinclair, and their assistant Greg Hadley stood windblown in front of the magnificent Carson mansion.

FATEMEH S. ROTH

It is through Art, and through Art only, that we can realize our perfection; through Art and Art only that we can shield ourselves from the sordid perils of existence.

—Oscar Wilde